SHADES OF HARMONY

Edited by

Steve Twelvetree

First published in Great Britain in 2000 by
TRIUMPH HOUSE
Remus House,
Coltsfoot Drive,
Woodston,
Peterborough, PE2 9JX
Telephone (01733) 898102

All Rights Reserved

Copyright Contributors 2000

HB ISBN 1 86161 753 4
SB ISBN 1 86161 758 5

FOREWORD

For many of us the medium of poetry offers us a voice - a voice to speak out and let others know what we feel, think and desire. It is the vital bridge of communication that lets us share our innermost thoughts and messages on life to people who may need that vital surge of poetic inspiration. It offers experience to those with none or little, spreads light to those in darkness and at the same time it encourages others that they are not alone.

Shades of Harmony is a unique collection of Christian poetry written in a variety of styles and on a combination of themes. The poems are easy to relate to and encouraging to read, offering engaging entertainment to their reader.

This delightful collection is sure to win your heart, making it a companion for life and perhaps even earning that favourite little spot upon your bookshelf.

Steve Twelvetree
Editor

CONTENTS

Title	Author	Page
Beef On The Bone ...	Nicholas Winn	1
Mr Jones	Graham Rippon	2
Nature's Sunset Picture	Mae Cadman	3
The Song Thrush	Nancy Solly	4
Winter's End	Ruth Dewhirst	6
A Visit To The Dream Factory	Louie Carr	7
I'd Rather Be Me	Ray Wesley Jones	8
Diversity	Ian Caughey	10
Awakenings	Doreen Wheeldon	11
Spring's Awakening	Isobel Laffin	12
An Anniversary Message	J Fletcher	13
An Honest Request	Rowland Patrick Scannell	14
Through The Rainbow	Sara Newby	15
Prayer For My Journey	Susanne Weber	16
A Drinker's Toast	David L Morgan	17
Long Awaited Season	Irene Hart	18
The Primrose	Helen M Seeley	19
Millennium Dawn	Judy Studd	20
A Gift Of Love	Barbara Wait	22
Angel And The Fat Man	David Tallach	23
A Season For All Things	John Harrold	24
The Magpie	Lynn Brookes	26
Love	Valerie Sutton	27
Eldorado - The Facts ...	J G Ryder	28
A Tall Tale	Eric Holt	30
Your Garden Awaits	Eva A Perrin	32
Along The King's Highway	Christina Miller	33
Untitled	Heather Hill	34
Plea Of The Grateful	Perry McDaid	35
Four Seasons	Sally Smith	36
Wear No Face Of Sorrow	A Branthwaite	37
The Causeway	Janet Hewitt	38
Why Do You Bother?	Margaret Poole	40
Dawn Over Lake Gennesaret	Lionel Reid	41
A Song For Spring	Marcella Pellow	42
The Hope Of The Resurrection	Elsie Norman	43

A Meerschaum Pipe	Christine Knight	44
The Vicar's Dilemma	Sue Goodman	45
The Mists Of Time	Iris Covell	46
The Doctor's Waiting Room	J Smyth	48
Hospital Admission	Mary Weeks	50
Polarised	Marylène Walker	52
The Joys Of Spring	Cathy Mearman	53
Colours Of The Rainbow	Jess Chambers	54
Winter	D Snow	56
Longing For Jerusalem	Marie Housam	57
Come Again	Evelyn Leite	58
Multi-Tasking	Ann Clifton	59
Pests	Eric E Webb	60
Keep Smiling	Marian Hunt	62
Palm Sunday	Madeleine Scott	63
Shipwreck	John Statham	64
Circles	Freda Grieve	65
He Is Risen	Charlie MacIntyre	66
The Millennium Resolution	Stella Bush-Payne	67
Spring	Gill Sathyamoorthy	68
A Grace	Di Bagshawe	69
Spring's Mannequin	Pat Heppel	70
Bluebell Wood	Geraldine Laker	71
Spring Song	Catherine Riley	72
Millennium Madness	Joyce Angel	73
God's Presence We Share!	Theresa Hartley	74
Christmas Gifts	M Baxter	75
I Can Remember	Lillian Derry	76
Eastertide	Benny Howell	77
Man's Final Winter Comes	Don Woods	78
My Thanks To God	S C Talmadge	79
Our Mother	Elizabeth Gallacher	80
My Heavenly Guide	S T Jennings	81
Butterfly	Pat Marsh	82
Those Who Live Alone	Shirley Wolstenholme	84
Lamb Of God	Eva Burton	85
Be With Me Father	Pearl Gill	86
Lord, Help Me	Lil Bordessa	87

Age Allowance	Ann G Wallace	88
Five Political Clerihews	Anne Sanderson	89
I Wish	Tricia Ravenstone	90
Evening Prayer	Maragret G Hale	91
Discipline Needed	Lachlan Taylor	92
Seasonal Thoughts	John Joinson	93
Brighter Days In Winter	Chris Jackson	94
Prayer In The Underground	Katharine Holmstrom	95
Untitled	C Fowler	96
Autumn	Catherine James	97
Twenty Minutes To The Pound	Elizabeth Smith	98
A Song For Rejoicing	Nessie Shaw	99
The Sweet Lady Spring	Jenny Eleftheriades	100
Trees	Olivia Wheatley	101
A Scout's Outing	Mary Ryan	102
Christmas Thoughts . . .	Maureen Richardson	104
Millennium Moan	Roger Carpenter	106

BEEF ON THE BONE, AND THE MOBILE PHONE

They've put the beef back on the bone,
Or is the bone back on the beef?
Why don't they leave things well alone
That cause the general public grief?
There's CJD, or is it B?
Mad cows, (and maybe bulls as well),
Genetic crops
Robotic cops
And neighbours all around, from Hell.

They're sending bits and bobs to Mars
To see if life exists, while we
Are swamped with lorries, queues of cars,
And gridlock, a reality;
Our latest pet, the Internet
Is creeping into every house,
Just prod or poke
Or better stroke
That plastic thing they call 'The Mouse'

And not forgetting one more thing,
Lest hi-tech, guru's quail and moan,
That little slab that doesn't ring
But shrieks a tune, the mobile phone!
In shop or store you'll hear it pour
Its sweet cadences far and near,
And then you'll see
One's loose and free:
And burrowing in someone's ear!

Nicholas Winn

MR JONES

Dinosaurs are dead for sure,
So who is that who lives next door?

It's not a rabbit or a bird -
One of those would be absurd.

It just might be that leering smile
Belongs to a suburban crocodile,

But crocs don't live in upstairs flats
Or go to church in homburg hats.

His door plate says he's Mr Jones
But his wheelie's always full of bones,

So I'm sure it's Tyrannosaurus Rex
Disguised in suits of woollen checks.

Am I right, or am I wrong?
For who could rant and rave so long,

Or stare at you with blood-red eyes
Like measuring up for oven size?

I'm told his temper's caused by gout,
But we both know his secret's out

And if one day I don't come back
You'll know I've been a supper snack.

Graham Rippon

NATURE'S SUNSET PICTURE

My cottage window seat expands the tranquil scene -
Of old stonewall - the garden swing - a cherry tree that leans.
Frames a picture, painted by the sunsets vivid glow -
Reflecting nature's beauty 'gainst the rivers gentle flow.
Now the sunrays spreads a sheen of burnished gold across
                                                     the reddened sky
Lengthening shadows enhance the shaded lawn, turns now a
                                                     deeper green.
Alters the beauty; but not the tranquil scene.

With darkening skies heralding the shades of fast approaching night
One by one the cottage windows reflect the fading glow of
                                                   evening light
Seated still at my window seat full rested now from rush of busy day -
Watching the beauty of my 'Nature's Sunset Picture' slowly fade away
As changing seasons alters the cottage garden scene
Each night the picture nature frames, a different beauty then be seen
Unchanging not our old stonewall, the cherry tree, the river running by
Enhanced by scarlet setting sun long shadows and darkened velvet sky.

Mae Cadman

THE SONG THRUSH

Perched on the bare tree's highest bough,
I catch a glimpse of him at last:
The thrush, who sings his heart out now
In gladness that the night is past.

Not once, but twice, each phrase he sings,
Some short, staccato notes, some long
Melodious trills, and each one rings
Out loud and clear, in strong bold song.

To see him walking on the ground,
With dull brown back, and speckled breast,
One would not think such varied sound
Could issue from him, with such zest.

Alert, he watches from the trees
The crumbs thrown out upon the lawn,
Then swiftly takes his pick of these -
My 'thank yous' for his song at dawn.

Throughout the day, he's sometimes heard
Tapping a rhythm on a stone
To smash a snail, or worm that stirred
Too soon - a meal he takes alone.

As evening comes, before he rests,
One hears the thrush's song renewed
As other birds fly to their nests,
Before he settles down to brood.

If storm or rain is in the air
The thrush sings loud and long, to tell
All who will listen to beware
Impending trouble. Listen well!

When overhead, the storm-cloud breaks,
Like other birds, he'll silent bide
Till it is past, and cover takes
Wherever he may safely hide.

Nancy Solly

WINTER'S END

Jack Frost grips all the land with fingers icy cold,
Cattle are snug in their stalls, and sheep in the fold,
And we huddle up before a cosy warm fire,
The nights are so long, and so easily we tire.

And in the early morning the grass is all white,
For it has been touched by the frost all thro' the night,
A blanket of fog comes down and is all around,
And as thick dense smog it hovers over the ground.

The snow is now falling, 'tis a wonderful sight,
Such beautiful soft snowflakes, so pure and so bright,
And soon the ground is covered with this soft wet snow,
All the landscape is white, and the north wind doth blow.

And even though all of the trees and shrubs are bare,
See how they are glistening in the sharp frosty air,
All around about is so majestic and grand,
And children play in the snow in this wonderland.

In their burrows and dens many animals sleep,
And our God in mercy His creation will keep,
Safe and warm in the earth till resurrection morn,
When flowers and leaves in their beauty will be reborn.

Animals will emerge into the bright warm sun,
Little lambs will skip and baby rabbits will run,
'mong the meadows sweet flowers and the fresh new grass,
For this dormant time of cold and snow will soon pass.

Ruth Dewhirst

A Visit To The Dream Factory

Edie, so tired she could have wept,
Laid her head on her pillow and slept.
Who could have heard her sadly say
'How I wish . . . ' just as she drifted away?

Edie went straight to the factory of dreams
And began to explore the various schemes.
Declining a guide, she browsed alone
And wandered into the *Partnerships* zone.
It was well laid out, and she was able
At a glance to read each label:
Business; Relationships; Dates and *Wedlock,*
And a section labelled *Deadlock!*
Eyes opened wide, she felt the force
Of a huge section headed *Divorce.*
Edie began to feel dismayed
By the plans so smartly displayed.
When she reached the *Husbands* section
She found it offered a wide selection,
And, on looking through range,
Was shocked to discover *Part Exchange!*

'This won't do! I've got my Willie;
Stubborn, overweight and silly.
We've had our days of grace and glory,
Yes, ours was a romantic story;
How this nearly bankrupt farmer
Was once my knight in shining armour.
'Willie The Great' we called him then.
To me he was a king among men.
I would not change him for another.
'Willie The Great Escape' - from Mother'

Louie Carr

I'D RATHER BE ME

Submerged in wealth up to the neck
Awed by the size of your salary cheque.
Burdened with, stifled by,
         options and shares
You plan your bright future,
         not theirs!

Seriously rich, what can compare
With your very own jet as you
         take to the air?
And having a chauffeur drive
         you to the city,
Surely it's others who
         deserve all the pity?

The higher you climbed though,
         the further to fall.
You had enemies all round and
         that was not all;
New bosses appeared, a change
         on the Board;
Goodbye chauffeur and jet, shares crash
         and you're floored!

'I'm sorry you've lost most of
         your wealth,
But your blood pressure's okay,
         you've still got your health.
Leaping from bed with that
         seven-am glow
To challenge the world.' You replied,
         'Well actually . . . No!'

'The stress and the strain has
                got me at last.
I'm on tablets, fast living's
                a thing of the past.
My wife has just left me, I need sympathy.'
'You've got it' I said, 'I'm a pensioner - poor
                but I'd rather be me!'

Ray Wesley Jones

DIVERSITY

As we activate our senses, taking the opportunity,
We discover all creation resplendent with rich diversity -
From the tranquil lake's reflection, so serenely engaging,
To the storm's unfettered fury, with the elements raging;
From the scent of the roses, attracting the buzzing bees,
To the birds' joyous canticles, high up in the trees.

Both the land and the seas teem with creatures plentiful,
From the ugly and grotesque to exquisitely beautiful;
From the most insignificant insect to the largest whale;
From the cheetah's agility to the crawl of the snail;
And from the flightless emu and the fluttering butterfly
To the grandeur of the eagle, majestic in the sky.

And the handiwork of God is mightily evident in all,
From the depths of the oceans to lofty mountaintops tall;
From the contours of vast canyons and rugged coastal scenery
To the spider's dew crusted web, of delicate intricacy;
From the parched, arid deserts to where the monsoon rains pour.
And from the small trickling stream to the thundering waterfall's roar.

Yet amidst all living things man is distinct from the rest,
Capable of logic and reason, with emotions blessed,
Of differing colours, temperaments and abilities,
But each made in God's image, given unique qualities,
And with a desire to worship, not easily pacified
Flowing from the God-shaped vacuum He has placed deep inside.

And the so called 'intellectuals' with maddening persistence,
Still vainly attempt to disprove Almighty God's existence,
Yet I with scripture's teaching my beliefs will align,
Gladly accepting the truth of creatorial design;
And spellbound by nature's beauty, its balance and precision,
I firmly assert that this 'fool' has made the right decision.

Ian Caughey

AWAKENINGS

The glory of the springtime -
The beauty of a flower!
Renewing nature's lifespan -
In every garden bower!

The fickleness of fortune -
When life is on the edge!
The hopefulness of nesting -
When birds begin to fledge!

Awakening from slumber -
And winter's cold dark hue!
The warmth of lifeblood stirring -
And passions born anew!

The magic of the springtime -
Is felt in every year!
As life renews its promise -
Its annual progress clear!

Doreen Wheeldon

SPRING'S AWAKENING

Spring is a time of awakening growth
When the earth comes alive after sleep.
Buds appear on the bare naked limbs of trees
And shoots from the earth do peep.
Pussy Willows bear catkins resembling chicks
Crocuses bloom amid fallen bricks
Snowdrops glisten with snowy white.
They sprinkle the ground with frosty light
Nodding heads like bells that chime
Spring's own messengers, time after time.

Primroses shyly take a peek,
From under hedges, fresh and sweet.
Ferns unfurl their fronds of green,
Asleep for winter they have been.
Now they wake, brown furled and shy,
Point their fingers to the sky.
Soon the bluebells growing free,
Spread a blue hued carpet like the sea,
Wave their heads in rippling rows
Like sea waves on a galley's bows.
Foxgloves point their spears on high,
Looking upward to the sky.
The yellow gorse in patches bold
Lends to the hedges, tones of gold.
Spring is a time of colour and hopes
From the country lanes to the mountain slope.
Let us enjoy it, too soon it is gone,
And another season has begun.

Isobel Laffin

AN ANNIVERSARY MESSAGE

It doesn't need a special day to bring thoughts
of you to mind
Because days I do not think of you
are impossible to find
But today is the anniversary of the day
I said 'I do'
When we stood together in the church,
the start of a wonderful life anew
I remember that special moment when I said
'I will'
You took a place in my life no one else
can ever fill
Through thick and thin, with our children together
we stood the test
Yet, now it seems too soon, God chose you
for his eternal rest
There must be angels at Heaven's Gate but it is
God who holds the key
And he alone knows the answers to life and
deaths' mystery
Each night I thank God for his love of which
I share a part
Also for helping me keep memories of you
forever in my heart
Thoughts of you are precious but did I *love*
and *cherish* you too much?
Because today (as always) dearest - most of all -
I miss your touch.

J Fletcher

AN HONEST REQUEST

Remove I pray dear one - with a ring of truth on high - the darkness that comes over me from time to time - I request, show me the light, that in turn will become brighter every time I pray - and look that my vision may stay clear as I endeavour to draw close to you dear God - Knowing in my heart and thoughts - I shall receive a balanced frame of mind - then when the clock by its sound lets one know another hour of life has passed us by - now at this stage we must learn to value and hold dear each passing day - of the gift of time - time again we cannot always have our way - to do right or wrong - whilst the one above can see value in all he has made to come about - no blame can we lay at heaven's door - God's reason for the gift of life was to be enjoyed and still we are told without a doubt - to keep days of Paradise close in thoughts and heart - our seat of motivation - that by the powers of Heavens - calm will lead us in the ways we should live our life - the statement made, I know best - can at times bring regrets - no values come from a sadden heart - leaving one with troubled thoughts and still with the passing of time - we can make an honest request to ask for divine guidance - throughout our passing years - of life.   *Amen*

Rowland Patrick Scannell

THROUGH THE RAINBOW

Drifting through the rainbow
On a cooling, gentle breeze
Bright rich colours envelop me
My mind is now at ease.

Silky red caresses me
Like blood flowing in my veins
Orange wraps around me
And yellow dissolves my pains.

Green like a rich, spring meadow
Cloaks me safe and warm
While blue as the summer sky
Becomes my soothing balm.

Indigo as the sky at night
Washing over my face
And lastly, sweet, soft violet
Reveals my secret place.

There I will stay contentedly
Until it's time for me to go
Then once again I will journey
Through the colours of the rainbow.

Sara Newby

PRAYER FOR MY JOURNEY

Dear Lord

When my journey feels like a walk
across the Rocky Mountains,
rather than the highway to heaven,
help me to remember
that You not only know the Way,
but are the Way.
There is no need to get stuck
in the valley of faithlessness.
With Your help,
I can move mountains.
Amen

Susanne Weber

A Drinker's Toast

I'll raise my glass to drink your health
With this joyful little refrain,
And when I raise my glass once more
Will you fill it up again?

I'll raise my glass to drink your wealth,
May your finance always soar,
And then I'll raise my glass again,
And have just one drink more.

I'll raise my glass to drink your joy,
May your happiness never sink,
And then I'll raise my glass again
And have another drink!

I'll raise my glass to drink your peace,
For drinking's not a chore,
Then will you please excuse me while
I slide down on the floor!

David L Morgan

LONG AWAITED SEASON

For long time now the frosty air
Has nipped our nose and chilled our bones,
North wind would seem forever there,
Howling, blowing as it moans;
Through the air and trees so tall,
Bringing snow and frozen ground;
A blanket of white seen by all
Who heard wind's unrelenting sound.

But now the snow has gone away,
The wind still blows, but not so fierce,
'Tis now the month preceding May,
No more the frost doth our bones pierce;
But gentle showers refresh the ground,
Once so hard like iron and stone;
Where sweet daffodils abound,
And birds do make their summer home.

The long-awaited spring has come,
The season bursts with life afresh;
Tadpoles swim, though caught by some,
The meadow wears her new gold dress
Of buttercups and celandines,
Whilst primrose in the woods break forth,
And birds arrive from summer climes
With others leaving for the north.

Only God can bring the spring
As His creation comes awake,
New zest to all life He doth bring,
As each new cycle He doth make;
So let us celebrate this time
Of new birth, new life and hope revived;
I am so glad that He is mine,
Who makes the earth to come alive.

Irene Hart

THE PRIMROSE

God spoke to me today:
there was no dramatic clap of thunder
that pierced my untuned hearing;
no meteor falling and bursting asunder
upon my mind's myopic sight seering;
no fire, no vision, no explosion.
But in the silent lifting of a leaf
and seeing there a primrose:
symbol of hope that goes on glowing,
new life after the winter growing,
from those pale yellow petals flowing
the beauty of God's faithfulness showing
the touch of His light in the world;
and in me;
for in that one moment, that glimpse,
my whole focus changed from me
to Him.

Helen M Seeley

MILLENNIUM DAWN

It is the eve before Millennium
a dismal, darkening December day
Time ticks towards midnight
and countdown has begun
Big Ben beckons, looming over London
The Ferris Wheel is set in motion
the Dome dominates a hazy horizon
excitement mounts
ending of an era . . .

No glossy calendars hang on Heaven's walls
there are no walls, no divisions
clocks, calendars being obsolete
bright party poppers, long streamers
strewn on special thrones
reserved for His return
during 2000 . . . ?

It is the Eve before Millennium sunset
God's golden paintbrush turns crimson, purple
indigo . . . nobody notices
the sun sets in a final flash of splendour
a blackbird chinks farewell from a silver birch
a murky mist sweeps in
the attendant mysteries of night slowly descend
people prepare to user in the new era
God watches from a distance
and wonders why man missed the real Millennium
As for the Magi - they just followed an eastern star
Earth's time ticks nearer . . . countdown
masses merge in Metropolis'
waiting for
Big Ben's bewitching hour
champagne corkscrews flung to
flashing fireworks
stunning as a sunset.

God has no watch clock or calendar
for Him no GMT
time is not measured
by square striking clocks
and round mocking clocks
His agenda is Love.

He laughs loudly longing for the truth to dawn
Man looks blindly into the distance
of a new sunrise

not noticing the sunset.

Judy Studd

A Gift Of Love

Alison, David and Matthew Paul
Went down to see the sights
At Blackpool, on the Lancashire coast,
Intending to stay four nights.
Alison carried Matthew, snug as could be.
He wasn't born yet, you see.
How could he have possibly known
A maternity battle was raging at home?
The Huddersfield, Halifax row rolled on,
As to where Mums should deliver their young.
'Stuff that!' thought Matthew 'I know where I'm at.
I shall decide where I'm born, and that's that!'

The anxious family, waiting at home,
Expectantly sat by the telephone.
There was nothing in Blackpool for Mum and Paul
Apart from a towel, and maybe a shawl.
The waiting relatives eventually learned
That, thanks to the hospital staff concerned,
They'd obtained the best souvenir of all.
David made that telephone call.

Most people return from a trip to the sea
With some rock, photographs,
Or a *Kiss Me Quick* hat.
This family came with a bundle of joy,
The gift of a premature baby boy.
Five weeks early is quite a long time,
But mother and baby are both doing fine.
Thanks be to God.

Barbara Wait

ANGEL AND THE FAT MAN
(With apologies to Johnny Cash)

There was a man whose paunch was equal to his height,
Then quite by chance he saw he was a sight,
A man fat as a pillarbox, without the means to run,
Living on his frites and on his bun.
He met a girl like none he'd ever known
She cared not for the wide waist he had grown.
And so he laid his buns down and let his body breathe,
Began living more economically.

But his old ways of eating wouldn't die:
Could not forget the chicken deep-fry.
And the food he'd had, both right and wrong,
Kept fighting for his whole
Till he felt forced to lick the soup bowl.

But now the old kitchen had lost its spell,
What once was tasty now just made him swell.
So the cookers, buns and bread knives in his life
Were out of place: and in his mind he saw an angel's face.
So he restocked his fridges in a day,
And the fatty food was done and laid away.
So he went out a thinner man than when he first met her,
And the angel got the fat man in the end.

David Tallach

A Season For All Things

A time to be born,
God knows what this is like
as he let Jesus be one of us.

A time to die,
he knows about this too,
as Jesus died for me and you.

A time to plant,
yes God planted his life
in with mine.

A time to harvest,
God's harvest will soon be
here, when we are gone.

A time to weep,
Jesus wept at the death
of a close friend.

A time to laugh,
Jesus laughed at James and
John as they walked with him.

A time to mourn,
Yes even here Jesus knew
the loss that we feel.

A time to dance,
Oh, how the Angels dance over
one repentant sinner.

A time to throw stones,
certainly, but not at each
other, or our friends.

A time to gather stones,
to rebuild the walls of the
Eternal city of God.

A time to kiss
and to also betray as one of
the Disciples did.

A time not to kiss
when you are sad and feel
that you are not worth much.

A time to get,
We need to get so that we can give
to others in their needs.

A time to lose,
all of our past mistakes,
when we give them to him.

John Harrold

THE MAGPIE

Dressed for dinner, black and white,
In best bib and tucker.
Looking dapper on the lawn,
Pecking some tasty supper.

Chattering with your feathered friends,
High up in the trees.
Showing off your gliding skill,
Landing on your knees.

Sometimes eyeing up the target,
As if out on a rave.
You go and dive-bomb poor old tabby,
So chums can see you're brave.

I like to watch you strut the stage,
In that infamous magpie hall.
Please do your party piece again,
The funny walk of old Max Wall!

Lynn Brookes

LOVE

What is love? God is love.
But where is God? Up above?
What is love? Where is it found?
Is it up in the heavens or here on the ground?
I love my husband, I love the cat,
I love the milkman, the one with the hat.
I love my children and what is more,
I sometimes love the chap next door!
I love this bracelet, I love that dress,
My son announced that he loves chess!
He loves his dinner and that's a fact,
I loved my job till I got sacked.
So what's the meaning of this word?
It's used too much. It's just absurd.

Valerie Sutton

ELDORADO - THE FACTS BEHIND THE FABLE

With flags and banners waving
The ship had slipped to sea.
Columbus, he had told them
'Paradise is what you'll see!'

But his crew were now revolting,
Well, they hadn't bathed in weeks!
What's more they had been forced to
Sleep twixt dirty silken sheets!

'Now come on Chris' the mate did say,
'Let's be sailing back to Spain.
I've got to do some shopping,
We can always try again.'

But Chris was not for turning,
For he had a stubborn streak,
Saying 'Nay, let's look at map again,
We'll find it 'ere next week.'

And sure enough they spied it.
'Twas just as Chris did vow,
It rose one morning with the sun
In a straight line from the bow.

The crew were e'er so happy,
They were packing bags with glee.
And as they rowed toward the shore
Chris bellowed 'Wait for me!'

By 'eck they were despondent!
There was nowt much there to do.
No swimming pools or girlie bars.
They didn't even have a zoo!

Instead they had a picnic
And played soccer on the beach,
While the locals jeered and heckled
Sitting safely out of reach.

But boredom overtook them
And the mutterings soon began.
They huddled all together
To thrash out a cunning plan.

At last someone was chosen
To break news to skipper Chris,
That they fancied leaving island
For 'twas nothing like sheer bliss!

'Now Chris' says chap called Carlos
'Paradise this surely ain't,
Looks nothing like in brochure
And we'll put in a complaint!'

'So the lads have all decided
That we're setting back to sea.
Back home to Spain we're going,
And we're getting back for tea.'

Back home with wives and girlfriends,
Reimbursed for their dismay,
They settled into work again
And forgot the holiday.

Eldorado was forgotten,
It had left Chris pretty poor.
He pulled out of winter cruises,
'Columbus Travel' was no more!

J G Ryder

A Tall Tale

It was the Tall Tales Competition,
For the teller of the biggest untruth,
Man after man had been lying all day
When up stepped a middle-aged youth,

'Pray tell us your story,' the chairman decreed,
'I trust that your tale has some merit?'
'Indeed sir, it has,' said the middle-aged youth,
As he fed a choc-ice to his ferret!

'I was lost in the Sahara Desert,
The snow was up to my ears,
My trusty camel had got the hump
And was crying crocodile tears.

Set upon by bloodthirsty bandits,
I was outnumbered a lot, if you please.
Was I afraid? Did I give in? You bet!
I was down on my knees!

They captured me, took all my money,
And tied up my hands, behind,
Then so casually, they chopped off my head,
They were not the slightest bit kind!

I spied my chance of escaping,
My faithful camel stood near,
I picked up my head, jumped on my steed
And soon I was safe, in the clear.'

The chairman had listened intently,
To the tale that had been so related;
One burning question he needed to ask
Before curiosity was sated.

'You picked up your head, with your hands tied behind,
That is indeed, a surprise!'
'I picked up my head with my teeth, sir!'
'Give that man the first prize!'

Eric Holt

Your Garden Awaits

Come, come my friends
How the grass has grown
Time to get cracking
Time to attend to the lawn

Take a look round the garden
And tend to its needs
Time to seek out
Those offending weeds

No good just sitting there
Moping and hoping
You know very well
Those flowers need coaxing

Reach for your hoe
And don some stout gloves
The roses need feeding
And so do the shrubs

So come on my friends
He who hesitates is lost
Those veg and those plants
Need some nourishing compost

Time to get out
Leave that old rocking chair
Your garden awaits
Your attention and care

Eva A Perrin

ALONG THE KING'S HIGHWAY

Please lead us Holy One
               I pray -
Along Your path
The King's Highway
               with You -
Help us not to go astray
But if we do -
O bring us back to You
That we may go along
               with You -
O Holy Lord and King
Along Your path O Holy One
               with You -
The King of kings!
Along Your Way
The straight and narrow
The King's Highway.
O Holy One I love you!
Thank You!
               Amen

Christina Miller

Untitled

Sweet sounds of bells, will soon be ringing out in
this wonderful world we live in
It's not just the end of another year, it's 2000
years since Christ's birth here on Earth
Treasured memories,
Now a bygone age - resting with Old Father Time
Let us not fear or ever take for granted the
beauty of all our Lord has made, and all that
we hold dear.
Accept His peace, giving thanks and praise for
love unceasing.
Whatever the future may hold for us, may the Lord
give guidance, strength, and hope,
And in love protect us may we protect, and have
all that the Alpha and Omega has created.
For Lord of all the years, our Good Shepherd
You will always be.
No plans I make, except for simple happiness
Tranquillity and peace and God's hand
Displayed in all.

Heather Hill

PLEA OF THE GRATEFUL

Lord, help me use free will for good,
Let not my weakness rule
to swing my resolve with each mood;
give me strength to be Your tool

May this mind You gave cease to dwell
on subjects which can maim
the fragile soul within this cell;
may I find peace in Your name.
Let not my sinning dispossess
me of the access home;
please, when it's time, let me rest
beyond gates where great souls roam.

Thank you for each taste, smell and sound -
for each glorious sight
with which this fine earth does abound,
Your touch and revealing light.

Perry McDaid

FOUR SEASONS

Springtime is my favourite time,
When seeds begin to grow,
Life comes again after winter,
And the seasons begin to flow.

Summer is a happy interlude
With its warmth and sunny skies,
Holidays that are sweet relief,
Away from stressful ties.

Autumn leaves start to fall
And vibrant colours appear,
There's a chill in the morning air,
Heralding the end of the year.

Winter has a beauty all its own
With crisp mornings and sometimes snow,
The quiet freezing evenings,
And stormy winds that blow.

Nothing stays the same,
For God knows how boring life would be,
So I enjoy each season as it comes,
And give thanks I can feel and see.

Sally Smith

WEAR NO FACE OF SORROW

Do not weep for me
I have only moved to another place
where death is nothing at all -
and slumber is tranquil and sweet.

Wipe away your tears,
life is for the living,
let laughter resound, now I've
left you for a while.

When long gone, may my memory shine.
Converse with humour and remember
the mindful smile -
and wear no face of sorrow.

My lamp still flames with brightness -
and be sure, it will forever
remain that way.
All is well.

A Branthwaite

THE CAUSEWAY
*(Inspired by a Prayer Meeting
Dedicated to Patricia Heath)*

The noontide was slowly ebbing,
On the beach we were sun-kissed,
The Causeway of shingle begging,
From the island shrouded in mist.
I was compelled to travel unaided,
A journey I had to embark on alone.
The islands' brume had not faded,
But I must reach my Lord's throne,
On the island, the Kingdom of God.
Fear of the unknown, uncertainty,
Was in each tentative step I trod.
I felt excited, but cold and lonely.

On the island ahead, I fixed my gaze
Where I knew my Father would be.
It seemed so far, as beneath the haze,
My laboured footsteps dragged slowly.
A heavy burden on the journey I bore.
My body ached as the island I neared.
Every movement was painful, a chore.
On dry land, suddenly the fog cleared.
I handed over my burden to my Lord.
Alone with God I talked, then listened.
He gave me rest, only He can afford.
On swelling waves the sun glistened.

Pure love, indwelling peace was mine,
As the Holy Spirit ministered to me.
In the company of my Creator Divine.
I wanted to remain there indefinitely,

But again the tide began to ebb away.
My friends were waiting on the beach.
It was time to negotiate The Causeway,
Whilst the mainland was still in reach.
This time I had no fear along the track,
Because my Saviour Jesus was with me.
I knew in my heart I would come back,
Just close my eyes, The Causeway to see.

Janet Hewitt

WHY DO YOU BOTHER?

'Why do you bother helping me?' the old man queried,
as someone cut down his high garden hedge.

'Why do you bother remembering me?' the old woman wondered
as she opened the letter that someone had sent her.

'Why do you bother noticing me?' said the old dog's eyes
as someone bent down and patted his soft brown head.

'Why do you bother loving me?' asked the child;
as someone answered his anxious weary cries.

'Why do you bother feeding us?' sang the birds, as they pecked up the crumbs someone had troubled to put out for them.

Then did someone answer them, saying 'Perhaps it is because long, long ago, someone gave up all their time and cared for me and so, remembering this, I willingly give unto you, my thoughts and my love just by offering only a moment of my life's time.'

Margaret Poole

Dawn Over Lake Gennesaret
(The Sea Of Galilee)

In silhouette across the haunted waters of the Lake
Where once our Lord and His disciples sailed,
A line of fishing boats is spread
To cast their nets at dawn,
Ere yet the sun has risen on the further shore
Still contained by dark clouds,
The remnant of night's cloak.
But now a glow appears and lights the sky
Behind the distant range of hills that fringe the Lake.
The stars have paled, and soon
A thin red sliver of the rising sun appears
To force its way into another early morn.
Slowly it gains strength, shaking off restraining clouds,
And turns from red to gold; and paler gold
As it clears the misty curtains of the dawn.
Then rising free of earth, the unshackled sun soars upward
Into a clear blue sky . . . The herald of another glorious day,
Leaving behind a golden path
Across the sparkling surface of the inland sea.
The rising sun, now in all its unveiled glory
Is but a symbol of that early Easter Morning
And of the rising Son of God,
Who is the light of this dark world.

Lionel Reid

A Song For Spring

Spirit of the living Lord
Our great salvation and reward
Come to us from they throne above
And fill our hearts with heavenly love.

Now in the springtime of the year
We surely know that Christ is near
Trees and flowers are blossoming
With beauty from our mighty King.

In the quietness of the dawn
While the day is still not born,
I kneel to thee and see salvation
For my heart my one oblation

Marcella Pellow

The Hope Of The Resurrection

Clear ring the bells as Easter hails the dawn,
Death overcome and human life reborn,
Robust fulfilling of that other morn.

The threat of snow in icy wind that blew
The drying leaves aside to bring to view
Defiant flowerings, that hope renew.

Ring out the bells! Defiant helebore,
Brave promise of a life renewed once more,
Now justified. Christ raised a conqueror.

Astonished unbelief concedes it true.
Forerunner of the faith of me and you,
That we shall stand again to live anew.

Elsie Norman

A Meerschaum Pipe

He was a chap of medium height,
His hair was thick, his eyes were bright;
In his lapel a rambler rose:
A Meerschaum Pipe clamped in his jaws.
A bloke he was of rustic ways,
He spoke most times in 'ayes' and 'nays';
But steeped in country wisdom, keen
To rationalise old nicotine.
His friends had told him - man and boy -
That smoking never brought one joy,
And, taken to its natural end,
Would be the death of their old friend.
Though told the weed would stunt his growth,
Relinquishing his pipe was both
An invitation to black mood
And good excuse to grump and brood.
Then logic hastened to his aid
And he a simple statement made -
'Without this pipe,' he said to me,
'I'd stand before you - eight foot three.'

Christine Knight

THE VICAR'S DILEMMA

There was a young Vicar from Brum
Who would persist in sucking his thumb.
Why did his voice falter
And his Sermon get shorter?
It was because he had a sore tongue!

Sue Goodman

THE MISTS OF TIME

Our lives are swallowed in the mists of time
We can only live one day at a time.
The present is here and then, O so fast
It's gone in the mists of the distant past.

Our childhood days once seemed so long,
Then suddenly we find they are gone.
These days have long been left behind,
Lost forever in the mists of time.

Our teenage years when we had to learn
The rules of grown-up ways.
We had our problems and happy times,
Now lost forever in the mists of time.

As you walk along life's road,
You may feel you carry a heavy load,
One day that load will be left behind,
Gradually fading in the mists of time.

We cannot cling onto the past,
It slowly slips from out our grasp
This past no longer it is mine,
Slowly fading in the mists of time.

The ones we loved and now have lost,
The ones we treasured most.
They too have all been left behind
Fading with the mists of time.

The energies which knew no bounds,
When we just loved to rush around.
They seem to be somehow left behind
Fading in the mists of time.

Every step we forward take,
Is a step into the unknown.
And every step we leave behind
Is slowly fading in the mists of time.

But memories are with us ever
Helping us recall in our minds.
The things that we have left behind
Floating away in the mists of time.

Iris Covell

THE DOCTOR'S WAITING ROOM

Have you ever had a seat in a doctor's waiting room
And looked at all the faces, full of misery and gloom?
You see a man who's reading, yet never turns a page
There's a feeling of anxiety, no matter what the age.

Then suddenly a woman comes in rushing through the door
And in her arms, a little child of maybe three or four.
The people turn and look at her and then begin to smile.
The gloom is gone, the cares replaced by their interest in the child.

The young one sees a playhouse and then a pile of toys,
Which the Centre has provided for all the girls and boys.
The child then spots a pop-up book and climbs her mother's knee.
The people watching try to guess, which story this might be.

The mother starts to read the book, when the child jumps to her feet.
She's had enough of stories, now she wants something to eat.
And so the audience concentrates on the antics of the child
And no-one hears the doctor, who is calling all the while.

'Have all you lot gone deaf out there?' his large frame fills the door,
'You're wasting so much time, you know, I'm getting really sore.'
Just then he sees the little child, who looks up at his face,
And there before our very eyes, a change of mood takes place.

'Hello there little girl,' he says, 'what have you in your hand?'
The child holds up a lolly, 'if you want a lick you can.'
The doctor looks bewildered - then chuckles with delight,
'My day was going badly, now things are looking bright.'

The doctor then addresses his patients, everyone,
'I'm glad you've come to see me, I trust you're having fun.
I hope you all feel comfortable, make yourself a cup of tea.
Now, who is next? Ah, Mrs Brown, take my arm and come with me.'

I think this illustration, though funny, may be true,
For children make us happy, when we are feeling blue.
All little things are precious, for they're sent from God above,
Who gives us little children to care for and to love.

J Smyth

Hospital Admission

I was taken in, shown my bed -
My name was written on its head.
I looked around the room to see
Who else was in the ward with me.
The other ladies warmly smiled,
But I felt lost - just like a child.
Nurse put a name band on my arm,
Which only made me feel alarm!
Would they lose me while I was here?
The very thought filled me with fear!
Suddenly I felt insecure
And wanted to rush out the door
And head for home and family
Before the surgeon got to me!

I looked around, and then I knew
The others had these feelings too.
We bonded in a special way
Facing adversity that day.

We all wore stockings that were white,
No blood clots - but they were so tight!
We shared our visitors and flowers
And chatted through the dreary hours
Each supporting one another,
Trying not to be a bother.

We were hooked up with tubes and drips,
Some had stitches and some had clips.
We tried to rest, but who could sleep
Amid the noise of bell and bleep!
Rubber sheets were too hot for me
So in the night Nurse made some tea,
But how I longed for my own bed
And some soft pillows for my head!

How glad I was when the day came
For me to return home again.
However kind, no one could be
Substitute for my family!

Mary Weeks

POLARISED

A polar bear sat, very polite,
On top of the Empire State Building:
Igloos and icebergs are humdrum,
So he'd taken this trip,
New York at his feet!

It was a hot afternoon,
And he sipped lemonade,
No ice cubes!

A policeman passing on an aeroplane
Had serious doubts about this bear,
Dirty glasses everywhere! Under-age drinker!

Closer, our polar bear was very sober,
His bow tie straighter than ever.
But he'd stuck bubbles on his fur
And was dancing light as a feather in the air:
He wanted to fly home for dinner!
                      Just another holiday-maker.

Marylène Walker

THE JOYS OF SPRING

Oh the joys of spring
Let heaven and nature sing!
As winter dies away
Everything comes to life,
Animals awake from hibernation,
New shoots peep out from under the soil,
Trees once bare produce green leaves
And the blossom looks such a picture.

I love the ripple of the gentle brook,
Water, a symbol of cleansing and new life.
We no longer need to wrap up warm,
The air smells fresh from the scent of flowers.
The best things of life cannot be bought -
Nature in its beauty is a gift from God,
The Creator of the Universe and the
Sustainer of all life.

Cathy Mearman

COLOURS OF THE RAINBOW

Roses scenting the summer air.
Poppies in a field of wheat.
Bright shiny wellies on a toddler's feet.
These things are *red*.

Marigolds in a fat blue jar.
A furry bumblebee in a foxglove bell.
Tangerines piled on a market stall.
These things are *orange*.

Bright buttercups in a meadow.
Daffodils dancing in a gentle breeze.
A hot sun shining in a summer sky.
These things are *yellow*.

New tips bursting on a hawthorn bough.
Fat buds thrusting through the bare brown earth.
Verdant streaks that colour the sunset sky.
These things are *green*.

Waves that dance across a sandy beach.
A speedwell opening to the sun.
Kingfishers flashing along the rippling brook.
These things are *blue*.

Thunder clouds massed against a mountain range.
A midnight sky sprinkled with silver stars.
Deep velvet curtains hung before a window frame.
These things are *indigo*.

Shy flowers sheltering deep beneath a hedge.
Jackmanii climbing up the wall.
Hyacinths blooming on my window sill.
These things are *violet*.

Colours of the rainbow,
easy to retain -
Richard of York
Gave Battle in Vain.

Jess Chambers

WINTER

Autumn has gone and winter is here,
bringing dark nights and cold mornings we fear.
Slippery pavements, icy roads and
sometimes falls of snow.
Why do we have Winter, I want to know?
But then there's Christmas to look forward to, with
planning, shopping and plenty to do.
After that it's New Year parties with lots of cheer,
a new start, resolutions made for another year.
Then we have Valentine's Day, and for some, it's
lots of flowers and cards, who from?
Pancake Day is when we celebrate,
so is Easter, with eggs and Simnel cake.
Winter goes quickly through the back door,
As spring comes in, with flowers galore.

D Snow

LONGING FOR JERUSALEM

I want to see
Where Jesus entered
Riding on a donkey
Cheered by crowds shouting 'Hosanna!'

I want to go
And follow His steps to Calvary
Where He gave His life
On the rough wooden cross.

I want to visit
Where He rose again
The stone rolled back
Triumph over Sin and Death.

I want to see Jerusalem
Where Jesus once walked
Blessing the people, performing miracles
And still He reigns today.

Marie Housam

Come Again

As yet we are darkly aware
these leaves are under,
fallen from their summer height
to surrender their gold
to the silver frost.
As we trample the paved way
yet we shall wonder
where go the numbers
tumbling to earth in the Fall,
and the whisper they whisper
into living ears, till the Spring
yes the Spring, bursts
the leaf buds asunder
resurrecting the day and
the Creed that reminds us
a tree is a tree is a tree.

Evelyn Leite

MULTI-TASKING

I wish I could divide in four -
I could accomplish so much more!
There always seems so much to do
And moments spare are very few.
The 'in tray' piles up day by day,
Expanding to the 'pending' tray.
Work overflows to fill the space
And life becomes one hectic race.
May I slow down and look around
Where nature's beauty can be found
And find new strength to face each day
With peace to blow the haste away.
For there is only one of me,
So I just press on steadily
Accomplishing tasks one by one
Until at last they all are done.

Ann Clifton

Pests

When God decided His earth was good He approved it, He loved it and blessed it.
The problem remains - not yet understood - who introduced pests to infest it?
Take the woodworm, for instance, a creature so small which leaves property owners distraught
Clever with destruction of timber construction and - in perfecting round holes well taught.

Attacking furniture and floors, skirting boards and doors, these ravenous pests bring disasters
A chair leg for lunch, they continue to munch, selecting the rafters for afters.
I know not, I concede, when considering the 'pede' is the 'centi' or 'milli' the pest?
They hurry and they scurry at such breakneck speed to decide which is which is a quest.

And how about bats? Are they friends? Are they foes? And just what in life is their mission?
Do they really enjoy their upside down pose? Are they stupid or just lack ambition?
With outlook nocturnal and features infernal they are tucked in secure habitat
Not truly a pest and when at their best could be loved - if you too were a bat.

After gardening long hours tending your plants and flowers massed armies of snails make invasion
With homes on their backs they form nightly attacks - come the morn there is sheer devastation
And despite good protection a varied selection doing well in the vegetable line
Is devoured by bugs, caterpillars and slugs though they too had no invite to dine.

At an earlier stage open warfare was waged against flies - green, white and black

Then - when it was thought the battle was won reserves of the blighters came back.
The fleas and the tics play unpleasant tricks whilst some species of spiders are spiteful
There's the dreaded approach of the voracious cockroach and wasps on the wing can be frightful.
The insects, elusive, we call silverfish, whose mercurial moves avoid catches
Dart here and there with a nonchalant air - abounding around in damp patches.
The penetrating song of the cricket goes on they seem happy to just be around,
Without making a racket the old leatherjacket does a packet of harm underground.

We are easily beguiled by rabbits when wild but by some countryfolk they are hated
Yet once in a hutch they love them so much - so - bunnies - get domesticated.
The list is unending so let it suffice by noting a few pests remaining
So varied, so virile and mostly not nice - no wonder there's so much complaining.

The house flies, the horse flies, bluebottles and lice, beetles, maggots and weevils,
Gnats and mosquitoes, grasshoppers and mice, then there's rats to add to the evils
The one consolation - all these varmints are small. Let's hope 'twill ne'er be the case
When the gruesome all grow some becoming quite tall - turning tables on the whole human race.

Eric E Webb

KEEP SMILING

When you are in the dumps, a smile soon changes things.
Can you resist a smile? And the joy it brings?
Lifts the burden from your heart,
Care and sorrows all depart,
Button up your frown and smile
Then pass it on.

Smiles were never meant to keep, they must be passed around.
They are terribly infectious, lots of them abound.
You can't keep them, that's not right,
You must share them day and night.
It will cheer and bless another,
Pass it on.

This old life can be quite grim, so keep on smiling
Even if your heart is sad, keep smiles surviving.
Smiles were meant to give away
Brighten up another's day.
Whilst you're sharing, you'll not lose,
They'll pass one on,

Marian Hunt

Palm Sunday

Jesus *chose* me to ride upon when He came to Jerusalem
The crowds cheered and waved palm branches.
Hosanna to the King! Hosanna!
I felt so pleased to be carrying a *King*.
That night in my stable I told the others my story.
They did not believe me.
I did, honestly, I did, and I can prove it!
When Jesus rode upon my back
It was covered with empty sacks.
Later, when they were taken off
There on my back was a big black cross.
It arrived there I know not how,
But some donkeys carry it even now,
In memory of that special day.

Madeleine Scott

SHIPWRECK

We live on a shipwrecked island,
dashed upon the rock of Christ by ancient storms
whose buffeting still bruises minds
that search for languid faiths.
And those who seek His perfect peace
must do so on the understanding
that peace is found only at the storm's eye.

The demon spirits of the world
are never exorcised by cool distaste.
The conquest of the soul,
triumphant over ancient brutal gods,
is not a victory for contemplative minds
balancing equations of the truth,
weighing the word of God in scruples.
The crucifixion was not caused by apathy.

When Columba set his sails for Christ
over the chilling waters of a pagan world,
the fire of his conviction
blazed across the northern hills
and rages on down fourteen centuries.
When Augustine left the sun and sanctuary of Rome
to bring conversion to the mists of ignorance,
he infected England with the fever of belief.

But if their legacy is ours,
and we the heirs of incandescent love,
our storm of faith must be the guarantee
our children's heritage from ancient saints
remains a shipwrecked island,
stranded on the rock of Christ.

John Statham

CIRCLES

Bright sun circle of orange
High in Heaven
Warmth to bring from the
Brown earth the seeds of spring

Circled frill of bonnet
That frames the face of infant
Walking with grandparents
Discovering the world anew
Through a child's round eyes.
Age finding fresh delight
In familiar things
Together a new century begins.

Rainbow circle arch across
Storm of black cloud
Colours to lift the heart
With a promise of light to come
As a new dawn breaks through.

Internet circles the world
Travel to the moon circle
A possibility for all
Century of change
Drawing mankind together in hope.

Freda Grieve

HE IS RISEN

Turn around, Child,
  turn around
The Lord is risen
  no longer bound.

Look and see, Child,
  look and see
The Lord is risen
  I am He.

Weep no more, Child,
  weep no more
The Lord is risen
  your grief is o'er.

Go in peace, Child,
  go in peace
The Lord is risen
  go in peace.

Charlie MacIntyre

THE MILLENNIUM RESOLUTION

Gone are the December illuminations of Christmas cheer
Gone are the fireworks celebrating the *millennium year,*
Gone are the little bubbles in the tall champagne glass
Gone are the magic moments when the old year did pass!

Gone are the lights of little church candles on the *millennium* night
Gone with the *resolution* for *peace* and put the *world* to *right!*
Gone, but not forgotten as we each held our twinkling light
Gone are past wrongs as the *millennium resolution* shines bright.

Giving thoughts for others and having time to always share
Giving love and forgiveness, respect for all, and to care,
Giving time for reflection for sufferers 'a silent prayer'
Giving our inner candle of light, power to the *millennium resolution*
e v e r y w h e r e!

Stella Bush-Payne

SPRING

Dark days of winter forgotten
Snow long since melted on the mountain ridge
Spring bursts forth in all its splendour
Warming the spirit within.

The sun's warm rays
Are checked by spring's cold winds
Yet still light penetrates the soul
And blue skies make me sing.

Yellow masses of forsythia burst forth
Golden trumpets wave in the breeze
Vivid tulips reveal their inner glory
And velvet smiles of pansy faces dance.

The woods have come to life
Hedgerows house the singing birds,
There's a song in my heart this spring
That goes far beyond all these words.

Gill Sathyamoorthy

A GRACE

Lord as we sit to this food -
Help us remember those with none,
Cheerful friends gathered round,
Think of those who haven't one.
May we not eat in indifference,
Think of how it came to table,
Give thanks for our every Blessing
To One humbly born in a stable.

Di Bagshawe

SPRING'S MANNEQUIN

Such pink loveliness brushing my window
As the cherry blossom scatters softly,
Pale pink confetti, Spring begins to throw,
It drifts and drapes the bare earth profusely.
Myriad, sweet, blushing flowers on high
Bedeck the tree in a crinoline gown;
Resplendence is short as the soft breeze sighs,
The frothy skirt frays, soon topples the crown!
In a last frenzied rustling the gown swirls,
Cinderella must forfeit her splendour;
As a mannequin gives a final twirl,
Now a quick change, a green robe for Summer.
More flowers fall, the gown drops to her feet,
Re-dressed in green, she's poised, Summer to greet!

Pat Heppel

BLUEBELL WOOD

'Ladies of the forest'
Wearing silver gowns,
Caressed by the golden sun, while
Verdant hues of fluttering leaves
Dance in the hazy beams.
Their feet stand
In a sea of azure
Ultramarine and sky
Bluebells
As far as the eye can see,
Gently swaying in the breeze.
Like spindrift,
They surge and swell,
Caressing the trunks,
A blue mist lapping
Along the meandering woodland path
Leading to the light.

Geraldine Laker

Spring Song

Noisy, screaming, diving seabirds,
wheeling in the skies above;
Sweetly twittering, rising skylark,
plaintive cooing of the dove.
All around are springtime voices,
responding to the warming sun;
all around on sea and meadow
signs of new life now begun.

But what of me, that beholds this wonder
of new birth come again?
Will I yield to my Creator to bring
new life out of winter's pain?
Will my voice new praises sing
ascending sweetly to my King?
Gladly, I surrender to the warming sun,
grateful for a new song in me begun.

Catherine Riley

Millennium Madness

We start a new millennium,
for many people joy and fun;
But what's it really all about
I look around and want to shout;
a massive Dome, antennae high,
A big wheel reaching to the sky?
Drinking all hours of the night
results of which give so much fright?
If one wants to celebrate
then three times over normal rate
for such pleasure you must pay
just to celebrate one day.
Don't get me wrong, I am as glad as you
to pass from era old to new.
Most people see a New Year in
Look on the old and all that's been;
Wonder what the new will bring
but me, I see it as a sin
when all the money spent on this
could help the needy, poor and sick;
2000 years since Jesus came,
I think it really such a shame
that during all this celebration
which will take place thro'out our nation,
not many give our Lord a mention
not many know His true intention;
So Christians, whilst we join the mirth
let's spread the news of Jesus' Birth;
Let's start the new millennium
Tell all about God's precious Son
Fulfil the task He has asked us to;
and never stop 'til His work is through.

Joyce Angel

GOD'S PRESENCE WE SHARE!

I pray sometime each day
Well I hope I do
Anyway
Even if it's just to say
'Hello' to God
'I love you
I know you're there.'
I ask Him to keep us safe
My family, friends and those of whom I care
When people say 'God Bless you,'
With them I know I share
The love of God
And I know He's there!

Theresa Hartley

CHRISTMAS GIFTS

We're giving gifts at Christmas
Gone on for years before
Why do we give gifts at Christmas
As in the days of yore?

The glitter and tinsel of Christmas
Is often overlooked by the fact
Just whose birth are we celebrating?
Our Lord Jesus' Birthday, the truth
                            is very exact.

Jesus received gifts
Of frankincense, myrrh and gold.
That is the reason we give presents
Which has transpired to all His fold.

It's Our Lord Jesus' Birthday
Our most important King
He deserves all the celebrations of Christmas
And all the bells to ring.

M Baxter

I Can Remember

I can remember, long ago
Christmases white with snow,
a roaring log fire, robins red,
the excitement as we went to bed.

We hadn't much money, but we knew
we'd receive of nice things, a few
but, the expectation was there,
'I wonder what has been put in
                the stocking I've got.'

An apple, an orange, perhaps a small toy
it was the wondering that gave us joy,
taking things out, one by one,
they did their best, our dad and mum.

Then parties were given at Sunday School
we did silly things, acted the fool,
played 'musical chairs', 'blind man's buff'
some, if they lost, went off in a huff.

Things have changed as time's gone by
the price of things has gone sky-high,
and yet, and yet, I really believe
most children are pleased with what they receive.

For, if the real meaning of Christmas is taught,
they'll learn of the greatest gift ever bought
that after the long, long span of years,
the Christ Child was sent to soothe their fears.

Lillian Derry

EASTERTIDE

Easter ends wintertime,
Once more the weather will be mild,
To venture out, both man and child,
For Easter means, holiday time,
If only for a short spell,
So it's easy, its welcome, to tell,
For now from the earth will produce,
Out of the roots, fresh green shoots,
Then with joy, spring is sung,
Happiness is ours because
Jesus, arose from His wooden cross,
The children for Easter begs,
If only for the chocolate eggs
When the day is bright and sunny,
We find delight in baby chicks,
and the Easter bunny.

Benny Howell

Man's Final Winter Comes

The winds are getting colder
Soon the autumn leaves will fall
The trees will stand forlorn and stark
As though they hold no life at all

And all the creatures of the wild
Small or large, quick or slow
Are making their preparations
For the coming winter's snow

Food is stored, nests are made
Sett and warren dug extra deep
To keep out winter's icy grip
During the future long months' sleep

Thus nature works its wondrous way
As the years move ever on
Yet tragedy awaits its children
Soon so many will be gone

For even nature cannot fight mankind
That's placed a blight upon all land
Laying waste both field and forest
Slaying wildlife out of hand

And yet no protests stop the carnage
As mankind's population grows
But Judgement Day is coming nigh
When man will reap what he now sows

The warning signs are all too clear
These man has chosen to ignore
So man himself will destroy man
And the world will be as it was before.

Don Woods

My Thanks To God

Dear God it's good to know you are there
That for me you really do care
Each day I put my trust in you
To let me do the things I want to
To keep me fit and happy as I go along life's way
Able to enjoy every single day
I like to have a talk to you
And this I often do
To share with you my troubles
Makes them easier to bear
Knowing you are there to care
Sometimes when life has been quite hard
I've asked for help from you
And luckily for me I've mostly got it too
When difficult times have come along
My faith in you has kept me strong
And somehow I have carried on
My prayers you cannot always answer
Some things are meant to be
But I could not do without you
So thanks for being there for me.

S C Talmadge

OUR MOTHER

Jesus looked down from Calvary's tree
And in His great love gave to you and to me
The gift of His own precious mother
Close by our side you will always stay
Gently guiding us on our way
Sharing sorrows calming our fears
Helping us in this vale of tears
Mary our own special mother
When we are in trouble you are always there
With a tender mother's loving care
Shielding us from harm's way
When we listen, when we pray
For you are our wonderful mother
The pure unselfish love you give
Help us lead the life we live
Let us try to be like you in everything we say and do
To be obedient to God's will
And your love our heart will fill
For you are our beautiful mother
Mary, Mother of every nation
Participating in our salvation
When our life on earth is done
You will take us to your Son
Mother of all mothers
Oh Mary, our Heavenly mother.

Elizabeth Gallacher

My Heavenly Guide

I've been a Christian for eighty years
And all through life I've never had fears
Of changing my living in any old way
I like speaking to God whenever I pray.

Though He never answers my prayers every night
I know that He hears me alright
I've asked Him for help many times before
And I know He will help if I ask Him for more.

Myself and family know that God is love
So we pray to Him and their mother above
We have a special prayer for her every day
So we will tell you it now if we may.

Dear wife and mother, your presence we miss
Your memory we treasure
Loving you always
Forgetting you never.

S T Jennings

BUTTERFLY

The dance of the butterfly
Sings of joy,
Sings of beauty
And of peace,
Mirrors the wonder
Of the transformation in our lives.

Within a dark chrysalis
A life lies dormant;
In a dark chrysalis which is so small,
So insignificant,
So tiny in the hands of the Creator,
As it hangs unnoticed and uncared for.

Yet,
Deep within, a caterpillar is dying,
Dying to self;
Changing
In the warmth of God's embrace.

Slowly, patiently, secretly
Being transformed
Until
In His own way and His own time
A new life
Is ready to be revealed.

And when the timing is just right
For the great Creator's plan,
The new life breaks free.
Beauty is revealed,
Created from the ordinariness of a dusty chrysalis.

Nervously at first,
Uncertain of the fragility of the newness which it feels,
Slowly, trustingly,
The wings of the butterfly
Open themselves fully
To the sunshine of God's love.
And as the healing rays of love
Strengthen those fragile wings
New confidence is born.
The butterfly takes off
In a dance of joyous celebration,
Radiantly reflecting back to the world
The beauty
And the love
Of God.

Pat Marsh

THOSE WHO LIVE ALONE

I live alone but you are always with me.
I am alone, but your face in my mind's eye I seem to see.
I never feel alone, your arms are always folded around me.
I am not alone for I know you are always there, and I can always
      reach you in a second with just one small and sincere prayer.

Shirley Wolstenholme

LAMB OF GOD

In mighty power
The waves roll in
They thrash and crash
Upon the shore
White dancing foam
Froths and abounds
And ripples up and back and round

The Lamb of God
With might and power
Comes to us daily
Hour by hour
His might is shown in gentleness
His power in his humility
He comes to us to give us life
We need no anguish or no strife
But simply open up to Him
To stand, receive and then to live
His way is holy, true and strong
And all of us to Him belong
We thank you Jesus
Lamb of God

Alleluia! Amen!

Eva Burton

BE WITH ME FATHER

Be with me Father, when I feel that You are far away.
Be with me, when I find it difficult to pray.
Be with me Father,
When the world about holds nothing cheery,
And when I am tired, depressed, or weary.
Be with me Father,
When I'm feeling anything but gay.
Remind me of the terrible price *You* had to pay.
Be with me Father when all around I find no love.
Help me keep my eyes upon my Saviour up above.
Take my gloom, my weariness, my tiredness and my stress.
Empty me right out Lord, of my sinful selfishness.
Take me to Yourself Lord, teach me *Your ways.*
Gentle patience, kindness and love.
This is what I pray.

Pearl Gill

LORD, HELP ME

Lord, help me to turn from being a Martha
when I should be a Mary.
To be open and receptive to the holy spirit.

Sometimes the world and its problems
threaten to overwhelm me.

It's then when I need to empty myself of
self bitterness and envy.
To let it all drain away,
refresh myself in the living water
which never drains away.

Lil Bordessa

AGE ALLOWANCE

Dentures soon in a glass will be,
Bifocal glasses will help me to see,
Knee length pants up to my waist,
And the toilet I may need in haste,

I will wear a hat on my hair of grey,
Use a bus pass certain times of the day,
Have a metal stick with a rubber tip,
Especially for my arthritic hip,

My teapot complete with tea cosy,
Curtains part closed because folks are nosy,
A chiropodist will chop and shape,
Hard nails and skin on my feet that ache,

I will turn up for appointments at the wrong time,
Then tell the doctor that I feel fine,
The cap on my tablets will be too tight,
I will sleep all day, stay awake all night,

My back will not bend to lace my shoes up,
Tea will taste best from a china cup,
On handkerchiefs lavender scent I will shake,
Every bone in my body soon will ache,

My pension will come and will not last,
Compared with those wonderful days of the past,
I cannot wait what a joy it surely will be,
When the age 'allowance' comes to me.

Ann G Wallace

FIVE POLITICAL CLERIHEWS

That old campaigner Tony Benn,
Most strident, obstinate of men,
Had he a mission to divide
The Labour Party from inside?

A thrusting man called Tony Blair
For older fashions did not care.
From left-wing standpoints he withdrew -
His only slogan: 'Make it new!'

The Russian Tsar, Boris Yeltsin
Was quite the opposite of thin.
The burly bear would totter along,
Especially if the vodka was strong.

General A. Pinochet
Left Chile in disarray:
He'd rather be in some dacha
Taking tea with Mrs Thatcher.

Margaret Thatcher -
No one could match her.
Love her or hate her -
Britain's dictator.

Anne Sanderson

I Wish

I wish I lived in a story book
And sailed the rough high seas.
And climbed a mountain on roller skates
And came down again on skis.

I wish I lived in a story book
And ruled the world as Queen,
With lovely jewels and pretty clothes,
I suppose I can always dream.

I wish I lived in a story book,
Where men were gallant and strong.
And I had a voice that was sweet and true
Every time I burst into song.

I wish I lived in a story book,
And could paint a masterpiece
Of a happy and busy farmyard scene,
With ducks and waddling geese.

I wish I lived in a story book
Where life was perfect and right.
Where the lame could walk and the deaf could hear,
And the blind receive their sight.

I wish I lived in a story book,
How wonderful it would be,
And I could choose to be anyone,
Including just plain old me.

Tricia Ravenstone

EVENING PRAYER

Alone I come to you this evening,
With my head full of the day's events,
Worrying over who said what
And what I said back makes me feel tense.

Clear my head of all the dross, Lord,
Cleanse my thoughts, help me to pray,
Knowing you are listening to me,
You know my words before I say.

Here I am Lord, waiting for you,
Cleanse me from my doubts and sin,
Help me to bring my troubles also,
Give me your strength and help me win.

Put your cleansing fire within me,
Take my fears and sorrows away.
'Break me, melt me, mould me, fill me'
Give me your blessings every day.

Loving Father how I need you,
I need your love, fill me with zest,
So I can fight for you, my God,
So I will do my very best.

All glory to the Father,
All glory to the Son,
All glory to the Spirit Holy,
All praise to You the three in one.

Now I will pray.

Margaret G Hale

DISCIPLINE NEEDED

I do not agree with this go softly
   with those kids who won't obey
for I saw that smacking did no harm
   way back in my schoolday.

I had the belt often from my parents
   and teachers at my school
this stung me for a little while
   but still I played the fool.

Families must have discipline
   or chaos will always reign
but parents must choose the proper spot
   when they administer the cane.

I belonged to a mixed large family
   where parents were both hard pressed
but they handled us with a firmness
   and we were never left distressed.

I have seen lots of deaths today
   with babies being shaken
those murderers shouldn't be near kids
   with this cruel way they've taken.

When my father gave to me the belt
   it was on my bottom bare
it stung me for a little while
   but I remained still devil-may-care.

Lachlan Taylor

SEASONAL THOUGHTS

The nights are dark, the air is cold
And the Bible story is retold
Those shepherds and the angel; bright
Three wise men and the star at night

It is a time when families meet
To share the feast prepared to eat
The decorated Christmas tree
With presents there for all to see

The children with unbridled joy
As they open every toy
But Christmas time is also sad
When we remember Mum and Dad

Then it's over, families depart
We wave them off with heavy heart
Another Christmas come and gone
The dark nights still go on and on

John Joinson

BRIGHTER DAYS IN WINTER

A cold and grey winter's day
Ice and snow on the ground.
Birds fly down, searching now
For any food to be found.
The children have built a snowman,
Used a carrot for his nose!
Daddy tries to start the car,
Forever hoping that it goes!
The lady slipped upon the ice,
Not too many broken bones.
A man sits by his little fire,
Cold and lonely, but who knows?
The lights in town so big and bright,
Christmas cards and presents bought.
The young lad sitting with his dog,
Later some shelter will be sought.
The postman brings inside his sack,
Some Christmas greetings for you.
The messages of Christmas time,
Are written there in black and blue.
At this cold, grey, wintertime,
There's a message warm and bright,
For Jesus, Saviour of the world,
Was born on that December night.
So stop and think about the meaning
Within the greetings sending peace,
Whatever is faced at this cold time
Our Saviour's love will never cease.
And He will, if we ask Him
Our every need provide,
Call out now and tell Him
He'll always stay there by your side.

Chris Jackson

PRAYER IN THE UNDERGROUND

You might not think that, in the tube, I pray.
But God likes public transport (seems to me).
He feels at home with people, day by day
And readily shares our lives. He comes to see
How we are getting on, and lingers here,
Wherever his dear children move or stay.
I know he travels with us, standing near,
Crushed in the tight-packed tube. Now who can say
In what disguise he mingles with our crowd?
Mute but insistent, calling us to know
(If we are not too deaf or blind or proud)
'Be still, and know that I am God. Now go!'

Katharine Holmstrom

UNTITLED

'Peace on earth, goodwill to men'
What does it mean? Say it again.
'Peace on earth, goodwill to men'
Though men still fight and will again.
God sent His son to bridge the gap,
To pay the price to buy it back.
The peace that once so freely flowed
Twixt God and man . . . a friendship true.
Goodwill and trust the love they knew.
Till man, so carelessly did break the tryst.
No magic wand to make men love.
No stolen choice to make men good.
But promise true . . . forgiveness offered.
Through His only Son, God has proffered,
'Peace on earth, goodwill to men'
Twixt Heaven and Earth. Let's shout *Amen!*

C Fowler

AUTUMN

Metallic waters of the lake
Reflect the gold dust of the trees.

Bronzed leaves layer the summer lawns
And carpet them to arabesques.

And young and tender springtime wheat
Is now a harvest valley floor.

Along the ridge the forest flames
As fiery red lights each black bough.

Our God is Lord of all the year
From springtime song to winter moon.

And through the autumn mist He comes
To start His warmth into our lives.

For His great love, like gold and fire
Shines out from every autumn tree.

Catherine James

Twenty Minutes To The Pound

It was Christmas Day in the Smith's house
And the turkey was doing fine
I was new to this cookery business
So had carefully worked out the time.

Then Grandma said she had a feeling
'That the poor old thing smelt done'
I said 'Oh no, that couldn't be so
It was due to be ready at one!'

Then, when she could stand it no longer
And insisted that *she* had a look,
I thought of the season of goodwill
But, after all, I was the cook!

In the kitchen I was enveloped
In a nasty dark blue haze,
Then I panicked - I'd never encountered before
A twenty pound turkey *ablaze!*

My newly acquired husband
(Anxious to prove his worth)
Said 'Now, don't worry my dear
You know things could be worse.'

He smothered the flaming turkey
And rushed outside with the fat
(Though now we are older and wiser
We know one should never do that).

The moral to this little story
And for any aspiring cook,
Is forget the twenty minute bit
And for God's sake go out and look!

Elizabeth Smith

A Song Of Rejoicing

Oh come, on this great day of joy,
My Son is risen from the grave,
Swing wide the gates and let Him in,
Ring out the bells in joyous sound.

Let heaven and earth join in the song,
The way now clear to walk upon.
Beginning there on Calvary's hill
He made the way now follow Him.

Again I say, this day rejoice
And join the angel song,
And know there comes another day
When joy will fill eternity.

Then heaven and earth will sing one song,
'He comes, He comes, the bridegroom comes',
And on that special day of days,
The marriage of the lamb will be.

Nessie Shaw

THE SWEET LADY SPRING

Who is this singing so early?
Why so joyous today?
Has cold winter vanished?
Is the sweet lady spring on her way?

Have you seen the violets deep in the woodlands?
Are there white buds adorning the may.
Why are you singing so early?
Is the sweet lady spring on her way?

Are the frogs back again, and the hedgehog?
Are the daffodils dancing and gay?
Why are you singing so early?
Is the sweet lady spring on her way?

Jenny Eleftheriades

TREES

Trees that are elegant
Trees that are gaunt.
Trees like a skeleton,
Trees an after-thought.
Trees that are whispering
Secrets on the breeze.
Trees that are a-dancing
Everyone to please.

Without the trees I could not live
They have so very much to give.
The seasons come, the seasons go,
But the trees continue forever to grow.

Olivia Wheatley

A Scout's Outing

Back in nineteen twenty-three,
Or so my uncle said to me,
A new priest came to his hometown,
By name, firm stated, Father Brown.
Yet, as my uncle loved to read
Chesterton's vivacious creed,
On truth of name a niggling doubt
Quite hard to really be without.
But none gainsaid the Father's worth,
So stout of heart, as was his girth,
Who knew he nurtured sick and needy,
Gave inner strength to strong and seedy.

Therefore, the townsfolk found no doubting
Their choice to lead Scouts' summer outing.
Upon one bright and breezy day
He, with the Scouts, was on his way
In chartered train, which chuffed on through
To lush green fields and features new.
They, reaching final destination,
Prepared without procrastination
To full enjoy the fun and games
That only pure exhaustion tames.

When later, waiting hometown's train,
On station's mossy banks had lain.
Tired bodies, resting, gave full play
To sounding off success the day.
All loathe to leave as train came in
And their journey home begin.
In carriages of polished wood
They long discussed what had been good.

But Father Brown discomfort showed
In an unbecoming mode.
Attacked by startled station's ants
Divested of himself his pants.
From opened window shook them out
In hope that this would cause their rout.
Another train that chanced to pass,
Just as the selfsame time, alas,
Caught up his trousers in its rush,
Left him bereft, debagged, to blush.
Some kindly soul on sudden whim
A Macintosh then tendered him,
Feeling sight of Long Johns seen
As one which not the best have been.

Sad, when this Father passed away,
Despite his kind works wrought each day,
Most remembered Father Brown
As one been seen with trousers down.

Mary Ryan

CHRISTMAS THOUGHTS . . .

I thought of Christmas and the nativity,
Of promised joy, families and festivity.
Bells ringing from church spire,
The smell of pine from an open fire.

I thought of Jack Frost and icy tableaux,
Of misty breath and blue winter shadows.
Of moonlight and starshine,
Of black velvet nights, and cold wind's whine.

I thought of ivy and mistletoe and tall fir trees,
And of men and women upon their knees
Whispering a prayer of hope,
That crabbed mankind on earth might cope.

I thought of presents, gifts to delight,
Of feasting, of crackers, of candlelight,
Of carols and choirs singing,
Of angels through the heavens winging.

I thought of a donkey heavily laden,
The beast of burden carrying a maiden.
I thought of shepherds herding sheep;
I thought of Santa, and children trying hard to sleep.

I thought of the baby lying in a manger,
I thought of Mary and Joseph who welcomed the stranger.
I thought of Jesus, the reason
We celebrate this lovely season.

That tiny babe born in a stall,
At His feet wise men did fall,
For He was the gift of God's own son,
Emmanuel, Prince of Peace, the blessed one.

He came to earth for our salvation,
Sing songs to Him with exultation.
The saviour who was once a child,
Walked on this earth all undefiled.

I thought then how once again
He soon will come as king to reign.
Let us now our homage pay
And look towards that glorious day.

Maureen Richardson

MILLENNIUM MOAN

The clock is ticking,
      The grains of sand are dropping.
The countdown to a new millennium
      Has no way of stopping.
My newspaper informs me
      There's one hundred days to go!
To be honest with you buddy
      I don't really wish to know.
There's a dome in London,
      A monument to what?
A war has just ended,
      In case you've forgot.
We think we're so clever, have we come so far?
There's still people starving, while some spread caviar
I'm sorry I don't wish to appear as a party pooper
I genuinely hope there's no bug in your computer!
But sometimes I think we've lost sight of what living means
When pop stars are Messiahs, and we worship beauty queens
We've come so far, we glory in our new-found wealth
But look again and you will see history repeating itself.
OK the clock is ticking
      But my friend don't you agree
It's what we do with time that matters
      Now and every century.

Roger Carpenter

INFORMATION

We hope you have enjoyed reading this book - and that you will continue to enjoy it in the coming years.

If you like reading and writing poetry drop us a line, or give us a call, and we'll send you a free information pack.

Write to :-
**Triumph House Information
Remus House
Coltsfoot Drive
Woodston
Peterborough
PE2 9JX
(01733) 898102**